Dedicated to Elon Musk,
for his love of Chinese poetry

FROM CHINA WITH LOVE

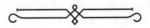

THE OTHER 19 MOST READ VINTAGE POEMS THAT MR. MUSK HASN'T POSTED YET

TRANSLATED BY JI CHEN

Skyhorse Publishing

Translation copyright © Ji Chen, 2022

All rights reserved. No part of this book may be reproduced in any manner without the express written consent of the publisher, except in the case of brief excerpts in critical reviews or articles. All inquiries should be addressed to Skyhorse Publishing, 307 West 36th Street, 11th Floor, New York, NY 10018.

Skyhorse Publishing books may be purchased in bulk at special discounts for sales promotion, corporate gifts, fund-raising, or educational purposes. Special editions can also be created to specifications. For details, contact the Special Sales Department, Skyhorse Publishing, 307 West 36th Street, 11th Floor, New York, NY 10018 or info@skyhorsepublishing.com.

Skyhorse® and Skyhorse Publishing® are registered trademarks of Skyhorse Publishing, Inc.®, a Delaware corporation.

Visit our website at www.skyhorsepublishing.com.

10 9 8 7 6 5 4 3 2 1

Library of Congress Cataloging-in-Publication Data is available on file.

Editorial consultant: Weihua Liu and Julie Ganz
Cover design by David Ter-Avanesyan and Weihua Liu
Cover illustration by Getty Images

ISBN: 978-1-5107-7230-4
Ebook ISBN: 978-1-5107-7231-1

Printed in the United States of America

Contents

Poetry

1

cáo zhí
曹植

qī bù shī
七步诗*

zhǔ dòu rán dòu qí
煮豆燃豆萁
dòu zài fǔ zhōng qì
豆在釜中泣
běn shì tóng gēn shēng
本是同根生
xiāng jiān hé tài jí
相煎何太急

From China with Love

A Poem Composed in Seven Steps
By Cao Zhi

Beans are cooking on a beanstalk fire.
Beans in the pot are a weeping choir:
"Why are you, born of the root we share,
Bent on scalding us with heat so dire?"

Tweeted by Elon Musk in November 2021

2

lǐ bái
李白

jìng yè sī
静夜思

chuáng qián míng yuè guāng
床前明月光，
yí shì dì shàng shuāng
疑是地上霜。
jǔ tóu wàng míng yuè
举头望明月，
dī tóu sī gù xiāng
低头思故乡。

Homesick on a Quiet Night
By Li Bai

Before my bed the moonlight shines so bright,
I thought the floor was paved with hoarfrost white.
I raise my head and watch the moon up high;
I bow my head and ache for home tonight.

3

lǐ bái
李白

huáng hè lóu sòng mèng hào rán zhī guǎng líng
黄鹤楼送孟浩然之广陵

gù rén xī cí huáng hè lóu
故人西辞黄鹤楼，
yān huā sān yuè xià yáng zhōu
烟花三月下扬州。
gū fān yuǎn yǐng bì kōng jìn
孤帆远影碧空尽，
wéi jiàn cháng jiāng tiān jì liú
唯见长江天际流。

From China with Love

Farewell at Yellow Crane Tower (on the occasion
of Meng Haoran's departure for Yangzhou)
By Li Bai

Leaving the Yellow Crane Tower in the west,
My friend is going downstream to Yangzhou,
Through the April blossoms and the flowering willow.
The lone sail now is a faraway shadow
and then, against the void blue, a nothing,
Save the waters of Yangtze that to the skyline flow.

4

lǐ bái
李白

shān zhōng wèn dá
山中问答

wèn yú hé yì qī bì shān
问余何意栖碧山，
xiào ér bù dá xīn zì xián
笑而不答心自闲。
táo huā liú shuǐ yǎo rán qù
桃花流水杳然去，
bié yǒu tiān dì fēi rén jiān
别有天地非人间。

Q&A in the Hill
By Li Bai

You ask why I have chosen to live in Emerald
Hill.
To which I reply with a smile of ease, but
wordless withal.
Peach blossoms, buoyed on the stream, sail into
oblivion,
Where lies another world, unlike the one of the
mortal.

5

lǐ bái
李白

yuè xià dú zhuó
月下独酌

huā jiān yì hú jiǔ
花间一壶酒，
dú zhuó wú xiāng qīn
独酌无相亲。
jǔ bēi yāo míng yuè
举杯邀明月，
duì yǐng chéng sān rén
对影成三人。
yuè jì bù jiě yǐn
月既不解饮，
yǐng tú suí wǒ shēn
影徒随我身。
zàn bàn yuè jiāng yǐng
暂伴月将影，
xíng lè xū jí chūn
行乐须及春。

wǒ gē yuè pái huái
我歌月徘徊，

wǒ wǔ yǐng líng luàn
我舞影零乱。

xǐng shí tóng jiāo huān
醒时同交欢，

zuì hòu gè fēn sàn
醉后各分散。

yǒng jié wú qíng yóu
永结无情游，

xiāng qī miǎo yún hàn
相期邈云汉。

(See next page for translation)

Drinking Alone Under the Moon
By Li Bai

In the midst of flowers a flagon is set
For a lone drinker with no company yet.
I raise my cup to the moon in a plea
That it join this party of three:
Me, my shadow and thee.
The moon is not one to know drinking;
My shadow tags along without thinking.
But for now, I shall revel with the moon and the shadow
For one must catch the springtide and move with the flow.
When I sing, the moon saunters to and fro;
When I dance, flail about does my shadow.
When sober, we make merry together;

When drunk, we finish and scatter.
Here, among the insentient revelers, is made a pact for eternity
That we shall meet again in the far realm of celestial infinity.

6

mèng hào rán
孟浩然

chūn xiǎo
春晓

chūn mián bù jué xiǎo
春眠不觉晓，
chù chù wén tí niǎo
处处闻啼鸟。
yè lái fēng yǔ shēng
夜来风雨声，
huā luò zhī duō shǎo
花落知多少。

Daybreak in Springtime
By Meng Haoran

From a spring slumber waking,
  surprised to find dawn breaking,
All around I hear birds singing.
With the wind and rain soughing in the night,
How many flowers, I wonder,
  have fallen in the lashing?

7

dù fǔ
杜甫

chūn yè xǐ yǔ
春夜喜雨

hǎo yǔ zhī shí jié
好雨知时节，
dāng chūn nǎi fā shēng
当春乃发生。
suí fēng qián rù yè
随风潜入夜，
rùn wù xì wú shēng
润物细无声。
yě jìng yún jù hēi
野径云俱黑，
jiāng chuán huǒ dú míng
江船火独明，
xiǎo kàn hóng shī chù
晓看红湿处，
huā chóng jǐn guān chéng
花重锦官城。

Welcome Rain on a Spring Night
By Du Fu

Good rain knows to fall in the right season;*
Now it is here, spring being the reason.
Carried on a breeze, gliding into the night,
It moistens all life, soundless and light.
Trails and clouds tarred by the dark,
The lamp on a riverboat is the only spark.
By dawn, the doused petals shall emerge;
Across Brocade City a sea of blooms surge.

*Quoted in Squid Game, S1E9.

8

bái jū yì
白居易

dà lín sì táo huā
大林寺桃花

rén jiān sì yuè fāng fēi jìn
人间四月芳菲尽，
shān sì táo huā shǐ shèng kāi
山寺桃花始盛开。
cháng hèn chūn guī wú mì chù
长恨春归无觅处，
bù zhī zhuǎn rù cǐ zhōng lái
不知转入此中来。

　　　　From China with Love

Peach Blossom of the Dalin Temple
By Bai Juyi

The fourth moon is when the floral feast the
world quits
Or peach trees start to bloom where the temple sits.
As the spring gone is sorely missed,
'Tis refound here, in a fortuitous twist.

9

bái jū yì
白居易

fù dé gǔ yuán cǎo sòng bié
赋得古原草送别

lí lí yuán shàng cǎo
离离原上草，
yí suì yì kū róng
一岁一枯荣。
yě huǒ shāo bú jìn
野火烧不尽，
chūn fēng chuī yòu shēng
春风吹又生。
yuǎn fāng qīn gǔ dào
远芳侵古道，
qíng cuì jiē huāng chéng
晴翠接荒城。
yòu sòng wáng sūn qù
又送王孙去，
qī qī mǎn bié qíng
萋萋满别情。

A Farewell (composed under the assigned topic of grass on a paleoplain)
By Bai Juyi

Across the prairie roll the lush grasses;
They thrive and wither as each year passes.
Wildfires may rage but survive they will;
When spring breathes again revive they shall.
Their scents, carried afar,
the ancient paths pervade;
Their hues, unclouded,
the forsaken city raid.
Here I am again bidding my friend goodbye,
The pain of parting
not by the verdure allayed.

10

lǐ shāng yǐn
李商隐

yè yǔ jì běi
夜雨寄北

jūn wèn guī qī wèi yǒu qī
君问归期未有期，
bā shān yè yǔ zhǎng qiū chí
巴山夜雨涨秋池。
hé dāng gòng jiǎn xī chuāng zhú
何当共剪西窗烛，
què huà bā shān yè yǔ shí
却话巴山夜雨时。

Writing Home on a Rainy Night
By Li Shangyin

You asked when I was coming home,
but I do not yet know.
Bashan's rain tonight is swelling
an autumn-chilled pond.
When can we trim the candlewick together
by the west window
And recall this night rain of Bashan
as a memory fond?

11

lǐ shāng yǐn
李商隐

jǐn sè
锦瑟

jǐn sè wú duān wǔ shí xián
锦瑟无端五十弦，

yì xián yí zhù sī huá nián
一弦一柱思华年。

zhuāng shēng xiǎo mèng mí hú dié
庄生晓梦迷蝴蝶，

wàng dì chūn xīn tuō dù juān
望帝春心托杜鹃。

cāng hǎi yuè míng zhū yǒu lèi
沧海月明珠有泪，

lán tián rì nuǎn yù shēng yān
蓝田日暖玉生烟。

cǐ qíng kě dài chéng zhuī yì
此情可待成追忆，

zhǐ shì dāng shí yǐ wǎng rán
只是当时已惘然。

Jin Se (The Lavishly Adorned Zither)
By Li Shangyin

Jin Se, with no rhyme or reason, takes on fifty
strings,
Each string, with its post, a reminder of the age
of bloom.
Zhuangzi the Wise dreams of morphing into a
butterfly of binary self;
Wangdi the Great returns in spring as a wistful
cuckoo from his tomb.
Above the sea of azure waters the moon shines on
clams whose tears become pearls;
Atop the mountain of Blue Fields the sun warms
the jade that oozes an ethereal plume.
What they evoked in me has become the stuff of
nostalgia,
But I was lost then, and little import to it I did
assume.

12

wáng zhī huàn
王之涣

dēng guàn què lóu
登鹳雀楼

bái rì yī shān jìn
白日依山尽，
huáng hé rù hǎi liú
黄河入海流。
yù qióng qiān lǐ mù
欲穷千里目，
gèng shàng yì céng lóu
更上一层楼。

Up on the Stork Tower
By Wang Zhihuan

The white sun retires behind the hills;
Seaward goes the Yellow River's flow.
To stretch your vision to a thousand miles,
Ascend another floor so your vistas grow.

13

wáng zhī huàn
王之涣

liáng zhōu cí
凉州词

huáng hé yuǎn shàng bái yún jiān
黄河远上白云间，

yí piàn gū chéng wàn rèn shān
一片孤城万仞山。

qiāng dí hé xū yuàn yáng liǔ
羌笛何须怨杨柳，

chūn fēng bú dù yù mén guān
春风不度玉门关。

Lyrics for the Tune of *Liangzhou* (Prefecture of
Cold Climes)
By Wang Zhihuan

The Yellow River rolls on, joining the clouds in
the sky.
A lone city stands in the mountains myriad
fathoms high.
O, shepherd's flute, why play the plaintive willow
tune?
The Jade Gate Pass is to the spring breeze
immune.

14

wáng wéi
王维

niǎo míng jiàn
鸟鸣涧

rén xián guì huā luò
人闲桂花落，
yè jìng chūn shān kōng
夜静春山空。
yuè chū jīng shān niǎo
月出惊山鸟，
shí míng chūn jiàn zhōng
时鸣春涧中。

Birds Sing in the Valley
By Wang Wei

No man is about, calm descends,
  petals falling, from osmanthus flowering.
In the hollow of the mountains, hushed by the
night of spring,
Birds stir at the moon rising—
  off and on, in the spring-lulled valley, they sing.

15

dù mù
杜牧

qīng míng
清明

qīng míng shí jié yǔ fēn fēn
清明时节雨纷纷，
lù shàng xíng rén yù duàn hún
路上行人欲断魂。
jiè wèn jiǔ jiā hé chù yǒu
借问酒家何处有，
mù tóng yáo zhǐ xìng huā cūn
牧童遥指杏花村。

Qingming (Remembrance Day)
By Du Mu

Pestering rain falls on Remembrance Day.
Heartsick travelers in a gray mood cower.
"Could you show me the way to a tavern please?"
Herdboy points to a village yon, where apricots
flower.

16

lǐ shēn
李绅

mǐn nóng
悯农

chú hé rì dāng wǔ
锄禾日当午，
hàn dī hé xià tǔ
汗滴禾下土。
shéi zhī pán zhōng cān
谁知盘中餐，
lì lì jiē xīn kǔ
粒粒皆辛苦。

Pitying the Farmers
By Li Shen

Farmers hoe the crop in the midday sun.
Down goes their sweat, dripping unto soil.
Of the food on your plate,
if you care to know,
Each grain comes from arduous toil.

17

liú yǔ xī
刘禹锡

qiū cí
秋词

zì gǔ féng qiū bēi jì liáo
自古逢秋悲寂寥，
wǒ yán qiū rì shèng chūn zhāo
我言秋日胜春朝。
qíng kōng yí hè pái yún shàng
晴空一鹤排云上，
biàn yǐn shī qíng dào bì xiāo
便引诗情到碧霄。

Ode to Autumn
By Liu Yuxi

The age-old myth paints autumn as bare and
forlorn.
But autumn suns, I contend, outshine the spring
morn.
Up in the azure, a soaring crane cleaves the
clouds,
Taking with it, to high sky, the poet's whim
reborn.

18

liǔ zōng yuán
柳宗元

jiāng xuě
江雪

qiān shān niǎo fēi jué
千山鸟飞绝，
wàn jìng rén zōng miè
万径人踪灭。
gū zhōu suō lì wēng
孤舟蓑笠翁，
dú diào hán jiāng xuě
独钓寒江雪。

Snowing on the River
By Liu Zongyuan

Of the many mountains, none has a bird in flight;
Of the many more trails, none has a soul in sight.
A lone boat carries an old man, caped and hatted
in rush,
Angling on the river, chilled by the snowy hush.

19

sū shì
苏轼

tí xī lín bì
题西林壁

héng kàn chéng lǐng cè chéng fēng
横看成岭侧成峰 ,

yuǎn jìn gāo dī gè bù tóng
远近高低各不同。

bù shí lú shān zhēn miàn mù
不识庐山真面目 ,

zhǐ yuán shēn zài cǐ shān zhōng
只缘身在此山中。

Written on the Wall of Xilin Temple at
Mount Lushan
By Su Shi

Seen front on, an undulation; sidewise, many a peak:
From near, far, high, low, each view is unique.
Yet the true face of Lushan forever eludes me,
All because I am here, in the midst of what I seek.

20

lǐ qīng zhào
李清照

bó wù nóng yún chóu yǒng zhòu (jié xuǎn)
薄雾浓云愁永昼（节选）

dōng lí bǎ jiǔ huáng hūn hòu, yǒu àn xiāng yíng
xiù
东篱把酒黄昏后，有暗香盈袖。
mò dào bù xiāo hún, lián juǎn xī fēng
莫道不销魂，帘卷西风，
rén bǐ huáng huā shòu
人比黄花瘦。

Hazy Gloom Rules the Day (An Excerpt)
By Li Qingzhao

By the eastern hedge, I drink to the gathering eve
As a quiet scent steals into my sleeve.
Verily blighting is this moment,
of a rising zephyr stirring the portiere,
And of me, a pining figure,
slighter
than the florets of the chrysanth fair.

League of Poets

曹植

Cáo Zhí (pronounced as /tsau jhee/)
(192-232 CE)

Cao Zhi was the son of General Cao Cao and the younger brother of Cao Pi, who became King of Wei. He was considered a prodigy by many, including his father, but his brother's jealousy and fratricidal vendetta cast a long shadow over much of his life. The story goes that at one point, by order of his less gifted, paranoid brother, Cao Zhi was to compose an allegorical poem about the fraternal bond in seven steps. If he failed, he would be executed. The sharp-witted poet survived the death trap with a spontaneous four-liner that has become one of the most recited and quoted of all Chinese poems.

李白
Lǐ Bái
(701–762 CE)

To the Chinese mind, the name Li Bai would conjure up images of a carefree wanderer in eight-century China drinking to his heart's content while composing poem after poem with his trademark flair and panache, among an ever-widening circle of friends. In fact, Li Bai's inimitable poetry and romantic, larger-than-life persona earned him the epithet of *shī xiān*, or Poet-Immortal (*xiān* being celestial, a mortal being who has outgrown the trammels of physical existence).

孟浩然

Mèng Hàorán

(689-740 CE)

Among Li Bai's many friends, one person stood out: Meng Haoran. They drank together, socialized together, and wrote poems together. If bromance had been a thing in those days, their friendship would have been its definition. Meng's life was a story of serendipitous encounters and missed opportunities, largely thanks to liberal imbibing and a recalcitrant rejection of sycophancy. His poetry is mostly about idyllic landscape, country life, travel, and reclusiveness.

杜甫

Dù Fǔ

(712-770 CE)

In the hall of fame of Chinese poetry, Du Fu, the Poet-Sage, is probably the only bard whose pedestal is as high as that of Li Bai, the Poet-Immortal. Initially, Du's ambition was to become a scholar-official serving his country, instead of arranging "the best words in the best order" in the comfort of his home or in mental seclusion. But destiny had other plans for him. His repeated attempts at a civil service career were scuppered, but a chance meeting with Li Bai, an established maestro by then, gave him a glimpse of the allure of life as a poet. Du's works, noted for their insightfulness and technical excellence, are a manifestation of the poet's humanity and an exaltation of beauty, friendship, and moral sensitivity against a bleak backdrop of war, devastation, and indifference.

白居易

Bái Jūyì

(772-846 CE)

Unlike Du Fu, Bai Juyi was successful both as an official (albeit with a four-year exile in between postings) and as a poet. In the former capacity, he was a beacon of integrity rising above a dark mire of systemic corruption; in the latter, he distinguished himself with outspoken critiques of political and social ails. Two long narrative poems, "Everlasting Sorrow" and "The Pipa Player," sealed Bai's status as one of the leading poets of the Tang dynasty. "Everlasting Sorrow" tells the love story between the besotted Emperor Xuanzong and his irresistible concubine Lady Yang, whose hold on the emperor was blamed for his neglect of monarchical duties, culminating in a mutiny that left the emperor with no choice but to order Lady Yang's death and the ensuing guilt that haunted him day and night and in his hallucinatory visions. "The Pipa Player" celebrates the gift and skills of a busking player of the *pipa* (Chinese lute) and laments the misfortune that had befallen her in a society rife with corruption, poverty, and injustices.

李商隱

Lǐ Shāngyǐn

(813–858 CE)

While Bai Juyi's scholar-official career was not all smooth sailing, Li Shangyin had a rougher ride as a bureaucrat in the strife-ridden waning years of the Tang dynasty, once a byword for prosperity and good governance. Li opened a window to the sensitive recesses of his mind by crafting intimately sensuous poems, some of which are highly cryptic, dripping in dense allusions. Of the latter the most famous is *Jin Se*, which, it is generally agreed, defies full decipherment.

王之涣

Wáng Zhīhuàn

(688-742 CE)

Quality over quantity is perhaps an apt description of Wang Zhihuan's body of work: A mere six poems by him have survived, and two of them are among the GOAT. Legend has it that he and two of his fellow bards were having a drink in a tavern when a group of professional singers came in to entertain a party of court musicians dining at the venue. Watching from the sidelines, the three poets decided to have a competition to see how many of their poems would feature in the performance, and the winner would be the one chalking up the highest tally. Wang was on a losing streak as the entertainers' repertoire appeared to contain none of his works, until the finale, when the most beautiful songstress of the band performed the highlight of the show: Wang's "Lyrics for the Tune of *Liangzhou*."

王维

Wáng Wéi

(699-761 CE)

Wang Wei (courtesy name Mojie) was a Renaissance man of the Tang dynasty, a poet, painter, musician, scholar-official, and Buddhist practitioner (hence the epithet Poet-Buddha) rolled into one. The fact that his works make up nearly one tenth of the classic "Anthology of Three Hundred Tang Poems," second only to Du Fu, speaks volumes. Su Shi (1037-1101 CE, see below) said of Wang Wei's genre-bending work: "When you savor Mojie's poetry, you taste visual art in the verse; when you regard Mojie's paintings, you see verse in the visual art."

杜牧

Dù Mù

(803–852 CE)

Du Mu and Li Shangyin (see above) are referred to together as the "Little Li-Du," significantly younger than but favorably compared with the "Great Li-Du," namely, Li Bai and Du Fu. His disillusionment with his civil service career, which had begun on a note of great promise, made its way into his poems, many of which are cast in a somber mood of determinism and powerlessness. But that does not take away from the fact that the genius in him composed many gems of poetry, often by blending contrasting images to create a lift or a liberating transcendence at the end.

李绅

Lǐ Shēn

(772-846 CE)

Compared to other noted poets of the Tang dynasty, Li Shen was first and foremost a politician, and a successful one at that: the highest position he held was that of chancellor. His political inclinations colored his earlier works, which are morally charged and worded in everyday language. Later in life, his poems became more introspective and expressive of his inner thoughts, matched by more ornate poetic parlance. His best known five-character quatrain, "Pitying the Farmers," quickly gained the status of a motto that resonated with a broad readership in a largely agricultural country. Even today, you would be hard-pressed to find a literate Chinese person who can't recite this poem.

刘禹锡

Liú Yǔxī

(772–842 CE)

Liu Yuxi was much more than a celebrated poet. His essays and philosophical musings are just as famous as his poems. His worldview was patently influenced by two Buddhist monks with whom he studied in his youth. As a scholar-official, he was twice banished, first for his involvement in a groundbreaking reform of the state machinery and then, a year after the end of his first exile, for writing a satirical poem, a thinly veiled dig at court politics. He was a close friend of Liu Zongyuan (see below), Han Yu (a preeminent poet and essayist), and Bai Juyi (see above). If anything could eclipse the Li Bai-Meng Haoran bromance, it would be the confluence of two poetic minds, i.e. Liu Yuxi and Bai Juyi, who exchanged reams of poems addressed to each other with outpourings of mutual admiration or commiseration, or both, till death did them part.

柳宗元
Liǔ Zōngyuán
(773-819 CE)

Much as the story of Liu Yuxi and Bai Juyi has touched many hearts over the last millennium, Liu Zongyuan and Liu Yuxi go even further back—they grew up together, worked together, and were banished together for their part in the ill-fated reform. It was during his exile that Liu Zongyuan wrote the best of his poems and essays, which recorded, among other things, his impressions of the scenes he saw during his travels.

苏轼
Sū Shì
(1037-1101 CE)

None of these biographical notes could do justice
to the amazing life stories of all those luminaries
whose brilliance has shone through the millennium-
long tunnel of time to dazzle and warm us with
their observation, eloquence, wisdom, and humanity
couched in masterfully crafted poetic language. And
this is even truer in the case of Su Shi, art name
Dongpo. Su was many things: a poet, essayist,
calligrapher, painter, politician, medicine man, and
gourmet par excellence. Suffice it to say he was a
towering figure on the literary and political landscape
of the Song dynasty, making a name for himself in
every discipline he lent his mind to. As a highly
principled centrist against utilitarian expediency
and quick fixes, Su Shi the politician was unpopular
with both of the opposing camps and his career was
a story of many setbacks with some purple patches.

He balanced his feeling of frustration with his prolific artistic pursuits and a keen interest in gastronomy. In fact, he purportedly invented a pork recipe (Dongpo pork) that shot him to culinary stardom.

李清照

Lǐ Qīngzhào
(1084–1155 CE)

Su Shi had many students. One of them, a high-ranking scholar-official, had a daughter named Li Qingzhao. Li was an avid reader from a young age and established herself as a respected poet in her teens, a rare feat for a lady in the patriarchal Middle Kingdom. She married a man who shared her interests, and many love poems ensued. Her love life was cut short, however, by her husband's untimely demise, a personal tragedy compounded by the devastations of war. The water-like feminine sensitivity and elegant tenderness that hallmark most of her early works are tempered with, in later years, steely patriotic outbursts, bordering on battle cries, which reflect her changed fortune and that of her nation. That notwithstanding, Li is generally held to be an exponent of one particular school of lyrical poetry characterized by elaborate and nuanced romantic finesse (*wǎnyuē pài*).

A Non-Exhaustive List of Basic Hanzi

天 /tiān/ Heaven/sky
地 /dì/ Earth/ground
人 /rén/ human
神 /shén/ god
气 /qì/ vital energy
道 /dào/ The Way/road

阴 /yīn/ yin/feminine
阳 /yáng/ yang/masculine
日 /rì/ sun/day
月 /yuè/ moon/month
星 /xīng/ star/celestial body

金 /jīn/ metal (one of the five elemental matters)
木 /mù/ wood (one of the five elemental matters)
水 /shuǐ/ water (one of the five elemental matters)
火 /huǒ/ fire (one of the five elemental matters)
土 /tǔ/ earth (one of the five elemental matters)

一 /yī/ one
二 /èr/ two
三 /sān/ three
四 /sì/ four
五 /wǔ/ five
六 /liù/ six
七 /qī/ seven

八 /bā/ eight
九 /jiǔ/ nine
十 /shí/ ten
百 /bǎi/ hundred
千 /qiān/ thousand
万 /wàn/ myriad (ten thousand)
亿 /yì/ hundred million

时 /shí/ time/hour
空 /kōng/ space/void

年 /nián/ year
月 /yuè/ month/moon
日 /rì/ day/sun
时 /shí/ hour/time
分 /fēn/ minute
秒 /miǎo/ second

春 /chūn/ spring
夏 /xià/ summer
秋 /qiū/ autumn
冬 /dōng/ winter
季 /jì/ season

东 /dōng/ east
南 /nán/ south
西 /xī/ west

北 /běi/ north

上 /shàng/ upper/up
下 /xià/ lower/down
前 /qián/ front/before
后 /hòu/ rear/behind
左 /zuǒ/ left
右 /yòu/ right
中 /zhōng/ center/middle

雨 /yǔ/ rain
雪 /xuě/ snow
风 /fēng/ wind
云 /yún/ cloud
雷 /léi/ thunder

江 /jiāng/ large river
河 /hé/ river (generic)
湖 /hú/ lake
海 /hǎi/ sea
山 /shān/ mountain

花 /huā/ flower
草 /cǎo/ grass
树 /shù/ tree
林 /lín/ forest

你 /nǐ/ you
我 /wǒ/ I/me
她/他/它 /tā/ she/he/it; her/him/it
她们/他们/它们 /tāmen/ they/them

世界 /shìjiè/ the world
国 /guó/ country
家 /jiā/ family
父 /fù/ father
母 /mǔ/ mother
姐 /jiě/ elder sister
妹 /mèi/ younger sister
兄 /xiōng/ elder brother
弟 /dì/ younger brother
亲 /qīn/ kin
友 /yǒu/ friend
男 /nán/ man
女 /nǚ/ woman
老 /lǎo/ old
少 /shào/ young

是 /shì/ yes
不 /bù/ no
有 /yǒu/ have/exist
无 /wú/ not have/not exist
大 /dà/ big
小 /xiǎo/ small

多 /duō/ many/much/more
少 /shǎo/ few/little/less
长 /cháng/ long
短 /duǎn/ short
远 /yuǎn/ far
近 /jìn/ near
真 /zhēn/ truth
假 /jiǎ/ false
好 /hǎo/ good
坏 /huài/ bad
新 /xīn/ new
旧 /jiù/ old
美 /měi/ beautiful
丑 /chǒu/ ugly

诗 /shī/ poetry